How the West Was Drawn

HOW THE WEST WAS DRAWN
COWBOY CHARLIE'S ART

LINDA L. OSMUNDSON

PELICAN PUBLISHING COMPANY
Gretna 2011

For my grandchildren:
Lina, Leilani, Hannah, Matthew, Melissa, Fynn, and
Wyatt Osmundson

The word "Pelican" and the depiction of a pelican are
trademarks of Pelican Publishing Company, Inc., and are
registered in the U.S. Patent and Trademark Office.

Library of Congress Cataloging-in-Publication Data

Osmundson, Linda L.
  How the West was drawn : Cowboy Charlie's art / Linda L. Osmundson.
      p. cm.
  ISBN 978-1-58980-884-3 (hardcover : alk. paper) 1. Russell, Charles
M. (Charles Marion), 1864-1926—Juvenile literature. 2. West (U.S.)—In
art—Juvenile literature. I. Russell, Charles M. (Charles Marion), 1864-
1926. II. Title. III. Title: Cowboy Charlie's art.
  N6537.R88O86 2011
  709.2—dc22

                                                              2010036749

Printed in China

Published by Pelican Publishing Company, Inc.
1000 Burmaster Street, Gretna, Louisiana 70053

INTRODUCTION

Reading this book is like taking an art-museum tour of the works of Western painter/sculptor Charles Marion Russell, known as Cowboy Charlie (1864-1926). For each work presented, you will look at the picture, explore some questions, and then learn about the piece's background. You can add to your experience with the writing, research, and art-appreciation activities suggested below.

Writing

Choose a painting. Use your five senses to get into the picture. What do you see, hear, smell, taste, or feel when you look at it? Write a story about what would happen next if the picture came to life.

You can also write down adjectives and nouns that describe the image. Combine them with *as* or *like* to make phrases, such as *colorful as a rainbow, dark as night,* or *sad like a hurt child.* Read out loud what you've written, with lots of expression. Guess what. You've written poetry!

Research

Delve into the period, researching clothing, food, transportation, living conditions, Indians, cowboys, and the Wild West. Compare the Wild West to today or to your hometown in the 1800s-1900s. A timeline of Russell's life can be found at the end of the book.

Art Appreciation

Compare Russell's works to those of other Western artists, such as Frederic Remington, Thomas Moran, and Albert Bierstadt, or of other artists of the period, such as Claude Monet, Georges Seurat, Auguste Rodin, Vincent van Gogh, William-Adolphe Bouguereau, Mary Cassatt, and Edgar Degas. How is Russell's work different?

Look for lines, shapes, and colors in each work and research the materials (watercolor, oil, and wax) that you see in this book.

Can you find an item Cowboy Charlie wears that is different from cowboys of today?

How many rings can you see on his fingers?

Does the figure look real?

A friend asked the famous artist Charles Marion Russell to carve a sculpture of himself. Charlie shaped the small figure with his fingers and fingernails from beeswax. Wax is soft, easy to work with, and looks like skin. It dries hard and lasts a long time. Charlie dipped the fabric for the jacket and pants in wax so they would keep their shape. Small metal pieces became rings, and string formed the sash. A reporter said it looked just like Charlie—his cigarette, his smile, the tilt of his hat, and his always-present sash. A friend said Charlie's "high heeled boots and sash were as much a part of him as his nose and ears." Charlie's sense of humor shows in this work. He gave himself a small body, large head, and big smile.

According to legend, four years after Charlie was born on March 19, 1864, the little boy "trailed behind a man leading a trained bear on a chain." At home, Charlie pulled the mud from his shoes and modeled a bear. That was the first of more than four thousand sculptures and paintings that he would produce.

In *Charlie Himself,* he wears a two-piece suit, dress shirt, tie, and sash. Cowboys of today wear blue jeans, usually cotton or flannel shirts, and belts. Two rings appear on his left hand.

Charles M. Russell
Charlie Himself—ca. 1915
Wax, cloth, plaster, metal, string, and paint,
11⅞ x 6½ x 5⅛ inches, Amon Carter Museum,
Fort Worth, Texas, 1961.58

Can you find a skull and a lariat?

If you were one of the cowboys, what would you hear?

If the picture came to life, what would happen next?

How did Charlie sign this painting?

What do the letters represent?

As a night wrangler, or cowboy, in Montana, each morning Charlie pulled his paints and pencils from his saddlebags and drew what happened in camp. At first, the other cowboys teased Charlie about his constant drawing. But when they recognized every man and horse, they hung the pictures on the bunkhouse walls.

If Charlie ran out of canvas or drawing paper, he drew on whatever was at hand. When he was nineteen, he painted this watercolor on a piece of cardboard he found in a package of crackers. Sometimes he shaped small animals from beeswax that he carried in his pocket. If he ran out of wax, he scooped up clay or mud.

Besides painting, sculpting, and illustrating, Cowboy Charlie told stories. Many paintings start a story. After we look carefully, we may ask, "What will happen next?"

Charles M. Russell
Roping 'Em—ca. 1883
Transparent watercolor on paper, 9¾ x 12 inches, Amon Carter Museum, Fort Worth, Texas, 1961.290

Can you find the tent with a man in the doorway?

What is the man's job?

What are the cowboys doing?

Is Charlie's signature the same as in the last picture?

The man wearing the apron in the doorway of the chow tent is the camp cook. The owner of one of four saloons in the tiny town of Utica, Montana, hired Charlie to paint this picture. He planned to hang it over his bar. If you "read" the painting from left to right, it looks like a comic strip. First a cowboy tries to calm a horse. Then a cowboy climbs in the saddle. Next, the horse bucks.

The *Helena Journal* printed this picture in its July 1891 issue. In later years, many of Charlie's works appeared in newspapers, either pictures alone or printed along with one of his yarns.

Charlie painted this picture on canvas. He didn't always have art supplies handy. The first time he painted in oil, he scraped a seven-foot pine log smooth so he could paint on it and used house paint instead of artist's oils.

Charlie changed his signature many times. Watch to see how it changes.

Charles M. Russell
Cowboy Camp During the Roundup—ca. 1885-87
Oil on canvas, 23½ x 47¼ inches, Amon Carter Museum,
Fort Worth, Texas, 1961.186

Can you find geometric shapes?

Find pictures that tell a story.

Find a peace pipe, animal skin, quiver of arrows, fan, and fire.

How has Charlie's signature changed?

In 1888, Charlie lived with the Blood Indians. It is likely that he ran out of the few art supplies he had brought with him and began painting on tanned buckskin. Friends claimed he even made paintbrushes by chewing the ends of wooden matchsticks or green twigs.

Years later, in this oil painted on a board, Charlie illustrated the inside of an Indian tipi just as he remembered it. A buffalo skin could serve as a blanket, coat, or decoration. In this painting, it tells a story. You can see charging horses and rifles, as though there is a hunt or war in progress. In most Indian tribes, men painted figures and women painted or wove geometric patterns on clothing and blankets.

Photographs prove that Charlie's new wife, Nancy, posed for this painting. Yet, the face is not hers. In 1897, this painting accompanied a *Western Field and Stream* story by William Cameron called "Keeoma's Wooing," and it became known as *Keeoma.*

Charles M. Russell
Keeoma—1896
Oil on board, 18 x 24½ inches, Private Collection,
Dallas, Texas

Can you find a small beaded pouch?
Who would have made it?
How do you know?
How are the Indians talking to the cowboys?

Montana blizzards caused problems for cowboys. With no landmarks such as fences to help them, they could easily get lost. These friendly Indians told the lost men they would find their friends on the other side of the mountain. This oil painting appeared in a book Charlie illustrated called *Mrs. Nat Collins: The Cattle Queen of Montana.*

As you learned in reading about *Keeoma,* women used geometric shapes in their weaving, like those you see in the beaded pouch here.

Charlie's pictures offer a true record of life in Charlie's times. The editor of the *Fergus County Argus* said, "Russell's paintings of Indian life and wild Western scenes have made him famous throughout the West, in fact all over the country."

He may have been famous, but he wasn't rich until he married Nancy Cooper in 1896. She bargained with buyers and raised his prices.

Charles M. Russell
Lost in a Snowstorm—We Are Friends—1888
Oil on canvas, 24 x 43⅛ inches, Amon Carter Museum,
Fort Worth, Texas, 1961.144

Can you find the man in a fancy hat from New York City?

Find the schoolmarm, the prospector, the Chinaman, and the widow Flanagan.

Which signature has Charlie used?

How is it different from some of his others?

Charlie painted this well-known robbery by an outlaw named Big Nose George. The holdup happened in the Black Hills of Montana. Big Nose George learned that Mr. Ikey had won a faro card game. Ikey had sewn several thousand dollars into his clothing. The robbers found it. In this painting, the man in the top hat and Eastern clothing is the card shark, Mr. Ikey.

Even though Charlie was not on this stagecoach when it was held up, he knew many of the people who were. Charlie eventually changed his paintings by using brighter colors and fewer people.

Charles M. Russell
The Hold Up—1899
Oil on canvas, 30 x 48 inches, Petrie Collection,
Denver, Colorado

Who is talking in sign language?

Can you find Captain Lewis? He holds a shotgun.

Find Captain Clark. He wears a triangle-shaped hat.

Find Clark's manservant.

How many boats are in the picture?

Has Charlie's signature changed from the last painting?

Even though Charlie never finished school, he loved to read. After reading the journal of Lewis and Clark's expedition, he was inspired to paint several important pictures. Here the expedition arrives at Grey's Bay (today in Washington state) with their guide, Sacajawea. One hundred years after the trip actually happened, Charlie imagined what this meeting with the local Indians looked like.

Charlie displayed his art at the St. Louis World's Fair in 1904. Later, he showed works at galleries around America and in Europe.

Charles M. Russell
Lewis and Clark on the Lower Columbia—1905
Opaque and transparent watercolor over graphite underdrawing on paper, 18¾ x 23⅞ inches, Amon Carter Museum, Fort Worth, Texas, 1961.195

Can you find the doubtful guest? Is he friendly? How do you know?

Is the Indian alone?

Can you find the metal trap, saddle, drying pelt, and river?

How did Charlie sign this painting?

This watercolor shows how a young Charlie and his trapper friend and teacher, Jake Hoover, welcomed a friendly Indian to their camp. Even though this was painted fourteen years after he lived it, Charlie had no trouble remembering the details of the scene.

Charlie changed his signature often in his early years. He finally settled on this one and used it for the rest of his life.

Charles M. Russell
A Doubtful Guest—1896
Transparent and opaque watercolor over graphite on paper, 18¾ x 22¾ inches, Amon Carter Museum, Fort Worth, Texas, 1961.139

Can you find something hidden in the grass?

Do you think the Indians are trying to kill the whole buffalo herd? Why or why not?

What kind of weapons did the Indians use?

How did the Indians make use of buffalo?

Charlie sometimes hid rabbits, grouse, or other small animals in the foreground of his paintings. In this case, you have to look hard to find the rattlesnake. He wondered why people who looked at his paintings never noticed his hidden creatures.

The Indians killed only those buffalo they needed. If they killed the whole herd, they would run out of food and hides.

This painting was so popular that thousands of color copies were made. Some appeared in encyclopedias. Along with *The Hold Up,* this painting hung in The Mint, a saloon in Great Falls, Montana, for almost fifty years. The owner sometimes closed the saloon so women could come in and view his Russell collection.

Russell painted many pictures of buffalo hunts. Each is different, so he numbered them.

Charles M. Russell
The Buffalo Hunt No. 26—1899
Oil on canvas, 30 x 48 inches, Private Collection,
Dallas, Texas

Can you find a baby?

Who decorated the cradle board and the woman's dress?

How do you know?

The Blackfoot Indians believed the sun to be the chief of the world. In this watercolor, the squaw offers her child to the chief. She wears a traditional dress and stands in front of a typical tipi. The cradle board snuggles her son and keeps him safe.

This illustration appeared in color on the cover of the June 27, 1907, issue of *Leslie's Weekly*. Charlie had visited the magazine's office on his first trip to New York City in 1903. He called the city "the big camp." Even though many New Yorkers bought his art, he still preferred the wide-open spaces of Montana.

What are the tracks in the dirt?
Who is the most important figure?
What time of year do you think it is?

Here Charlie painted a Blackfoot Indian camp as it traveled to find fall hunting grounds. Whenever a scout spread the word of a buffalo sighting, everyone would prepare to leave.

Women gathered the household belongings and wrapped small children in the folds of their buffalo robes or in a cradle board. Boys prepared the horses. Men chose which horse to ride, got their weapons, and surrounded the women, children, and older people to protect them. Ready to move in an hour or so, they all followed the medicine man over trails left by wagon trains.

The medicine man's many jobs ranged from healing the sick to leading the tribe to new hunting grounds to making sure people told the truth. He also kept the sacred medicine pipe, which was believed to have been given to the tribe by the Sun God.

Charles M. Russell
The Medicine Man—1908
Oil on canvas, 30 x 48⅛ inches, Amon Carter Museum,
Fort Worth, Texas, 1961.171

Can you find who is from the East?

How does the Eastern woman dress differently from Indian and Western women of that time?

What is the cowboy thinking?

In this picture, Charlie tells us a story with pencil and watercolor. Unlike women of the West, this Eastern woman carries a parasol. Prairie women did not have time to worry about getting suntanned.

The first time Charlie visited New York City, he looked and felt out of place. He wore his cowboy hat, boots, and red sash. When Charlie told his tales, however, New Yorkers forgot about how he looked. Although Charlie traveled as far as Europe, he never changed his style of clothing.

Charles M. Russell
When East Meets West—ca. 1907
Transparent and opaque watercolor and graphite on paper,
12½ x 19⅝ inches, Amon Carter Museum, Fort Worth,
Texas, 1961.132

April 20 1914

Friend Sid
        I went up to the
Palace the other day
where King Gorg camps
every thing was so quiet
I think Gorg over slept
that morning
maby he was up late
in a stud game
any how I dident disturb
him
but took of my hat to the gard
an let it go at that
its a sinch that Gorg will
be sum sore when he finds
I pased with out calling
these gards are about as
fancy a bunch of bulls
as I ever saw
all six footers riged in
gold an polished steel
each rider stands at his
post like a statue
an if it hadent been for
the twich of there horses ears
I'd bet it was taxidurnist work
Tell Jim or Jinny Lanihan I was
going over to that Iland of theres but
I here those people have left the reservation
an are all out in hills making medison
if I could locate old Chief O Kellys camp I'd feel safe
but its a new range to me an I dont like to take chances

I stand all right
with the Irish in
Montana
but in there native
land they might
peg me for a stool
pigon
well Sid I shure
am lonsum
I wish right now
I had my elbow
on your bar
with a couple of
swallows of malt
before me
an sum of the old
bunch around
I'd surtenly loosen
up som talk
If I stay in this
camp long
I'l start talking
to my self
with regards
to your Mrs an
the bunch
Your friend
C M Russell

Address
Dore Gallery
35 New Bond St
London
England

Can you find where Charlie was when he wrote this letter?

Is Charlie in this picture?

How do you know?

In 1914, Charlie exhibited some artworks in London, England. He wrote this letter to his friend Sid Willis after visiting Buckingham Palace. If you read it, you will learn what he thought about the guards.

Charlie spelled words the way they sounded to him, so there were many errors in his letters. Some words were simply spelled differently at the time than they are now.

Charlie's letters were very entertaining, and he almost always included a picture, either in the margin, on the envelope, or taking up most of the page like this one. Here he even depicted himself. You can see his sash and wide-brimmed hat. When Charlie became famous, his friends wished they had saved all his illustrated letters.

Charles M. Russell
Friend Sid—[Sid S. Willis]—1914
Watercolor, ink, and graphite on paper, 6½ x 8⅞ inches,
Amon Carter Museum, Fort Worth, Texas, 1961.302

CHRONOLOGY

March 19, 1864—Charles Marion Russell is born in Oak Hill, Missouri, the second son of five boys and one girl.

1868—At age four, he sculpts a bear with mud from his shoes.

1874—At age ten, Russell receives a pony and plays his favorite game, Trappers and Indians.

1876—At age twelve, he wins a blue ribbon at the St. Louis Country Fair for a drawing.

1879—Russell attends military school for one term—Burlington College in Burlington, New Jersey.

1880—He is sent to Montana for a summer job on a sheep ranch. He quits and joins hunter and trapper Jake Hoover.

1882-93—Russell visits his parents in St. Louis. He returns with his cousin, who dies in two weeks of mountain fever. Russell works as a night wrangler. He paints during the day and gives his pictures away.

1885—He paints his first commissioned work, using house paint on a pine log.

1887—Russell makes his first lithograph of a painting.

1888—He lives with Blood Indians for six months.

1893—Russell quits "singing" to horses and exhibits a painting at the Chicago World's Fair.

1896—He marries Nancy Cooper.

1897—The Russells move to Great Falls, Montana. Cowboy Charlie's first story is published, with three illustrations.

1903-4—He visits St. Louis to introduce Nancy to his parents and exhibit *The Hold Up* and *The Buffalo Hunt No. 26* at the St. Louis World's Fair. He travels to New York City and meets cowboy humorist Will Rogers. Russell casts his first bronze sculpture.

1911—He puts on a one-man art show in New York called "The West that Has Passed."

1912—Russell exhibits at the Calgary Stampede.

1914—He travels to London.

1916—The Russells adopt a son, Jack.

1921—Russell sells a painting for $10,000, the most ever paid to a living artist at that time.

1923—He develops a serious illness, revealing a weak heart.

1926—Russell receives his last and biggest commission, for $30,000, in Los Angeles.

October 24, 1926—He dies of a heart attack in Great Falls, Montana.

1927—The Montana legislature authorizes a statue of Russell to be installed in Washington, D.C.

March 19, 1964—A U.S. stamp is issued in honor of his 100th birthday.